ROOTS AND WINGS OF FAITH

VINCENT G. DE YOUNG

ROOTS AND WINGS OF FAITH

Copyright © 2019 by Vincent G. De Young

Library of Congress Control Number: 2019941723

De Young, Vince. G. – 1938–

ROOTS AND WINGS OF FAITH

ISBN 978-1-950839-01-8

Subject Codes and Description: 1) REL116000 - Religion/Religious Intolerance, Persecution & Conflict 2) REL015000 - Religion/Christianity/History 3) REL012030 Religion/Christian Living/Family & Relationships

All rights reserved, including the right to reproduce this book or any part thereof in any form, except for inclusion of brief quotations in a review, without the written permission of GlobalEdAdvancePRESS and the author.

Cover by GlobalGraphics

Printed in Australia, Brazil, France, Canada, China, EU, Germany, Italy, Poland, Spain, UK, (3) sites USA. and available on the Espresso Book Machine© worldwide.

The Press does not have ownership of the contents of a book; this is the author's work and the author owns the copyright. All theory, concepts, constructs, and perspectives are those of the author and not necessarily the Press. They are presented for open and free discussion of the issues involved. All comments and feedback should be directed to the Email: [comments4author@aol.com] and the comments will be forwarded to the author for response.

Order books from www.gea-books.com/bookstore/, from the author vdylaw@gmail.com, or any place good books are sold.

Published by

GreenWine Family Books™

A division of GlobalEdAdvancePress

www.gea-books.com

DEDICATION

With great affection, this work
Is dedicated to my Father

Henry DeJonge

Born Hendrik de Jonge,
April 12, 1903
In the small Town of Smilde,
Province of Drenthe,
The Netherlands.
I admired my father's great faith
And can sum up His eighty-six years
on earth in four words:

"HE FEARED THE LORD!"

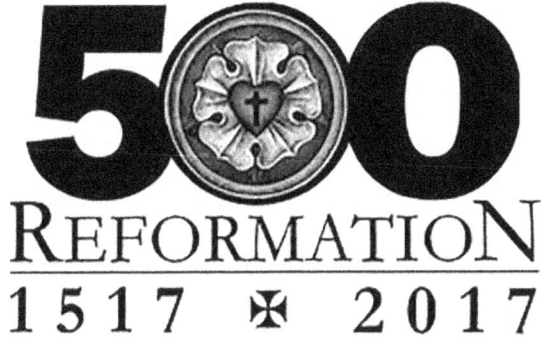

The 500th Anniversary for the Reformation was celebrated in 2017. It was October 31, 1517 when Martin Luther defiantly posted a copy of his 95 Theses on the door of the Wittenberg Castle Church. Luther's action was a spark that set the fires of the Reformation across Europe. At this period in history, there were many factors that called for efforts to restructure Church doctrines and practices in Europe. Luther was at the fore front of these efforts.

During the 1500s and 1600s, numerous people, local congregations, and countries were spurred on by Reformation ideas that broke with the established powers of the Catholic Church. The **Dutch Reformed Church** was created during this incredibly tumultuous period of European History.

Roots and Wings of Faith

Table of Contents

Author's Preface	11
Introduction	15
I. Reformation and Roots	19
II. Calvinism and the Netherlands	23
III. Resistance and Persecution	27
IV. Spanish and the Inquisition	31
V. Dutch Victory	39
VI. Dragonnades and Huguenots	45
VII. Christians of the Desert	49
VIII. Scripture, Faith, Good Works	53
IX. Persecution and Protestants	57
X. Creeds and Reformed Churches	61
XI. Hymns and the Reformation	67
XII. Persecutions and Meaning	73
About the Author	79
Afterword	81
Publisher's Appendix: Bible Translations And Differences	85
Suggested Reading And References Bibliography	93
A Word of Blessing	95

Author's Preface

My Search for Roots

The search effort to find my roots and wings of faith, started with a small event. An occasional painless tickle in my throat would not go away. What followed were many visits to physicians, a biopsy of lung tissue, multiple scans, and major surgery to remove a large part of one lung in 2014. The aftermath was worse than the surgery and during months of recovery, it sank in that my life on earth could end soon. Knowing my life had many days of good health, blessings and forgiveness, an incomplete thought stirred in my head, *"Why not write these things down so others will know and be encouraged that God gives purpose, meaning, blessings and forgiveness to each short life. And do it while there is time."*

With this motivation, the search of this heritage could begin, discovering values and meaning and answering the question, how did and how should these roots of faith and family heritage affect the course of my life, family and career.

When back on my feet, the story of God's Grace started by piecing together my parents' immigrant background. Realization became clear that little was known about the origins of the place where my family worshiped during my growing years. The Christian Reformed Church had roots in the Netherlands some 500 years ago. Church history courses had not taught the details of the painful struggles, the persistent fight for truth, and the incredible persecution against early Protestants. In my younger days, the meaning of that history never registered, making me a latecomer in learning the value and historic meaning of heritage rooted in the Reformation.

Although personal ancestry and DNA history are popular today, few have the desire to search for their "values heritage" or find answers to relevant questions; such as, what did their ancestors believe, what principles guided their lives, what impact did this heritage have on their life? This book records part of my search to discover my heritage and to answer the question: *what effect did my roots of faith and family heritage have on my life and career?*

The Reformation is a valuable source of that heritage. Its great value arises in part from the way it happened and the pathway of struggle with a formidable world power – a power that seemed invincible. For many years the populace was discouraged by that power from possessing Holy Scripture on their own, especially in their own language.* The main intent claimed for these restrictions was to prevent heresy due to incorrect translations, but the reformers did not accept this explanation. The iron chains of these restrictions were permanently broken by the Reformation.

***Decree of the Council of Toulouse (1229 C.E.)**: "We prohibit also that the laity should be permitted to have the books of the Old or New Testament; but we most strictly forbid their having any translation of these books.*

AUTHOR'S PREFACE

Beginning many generations ago, this story is about faith and fiery trials that, as taught in Scripture, produced character in those who suffered. That character in turn gave permanent life and hope to the Protestant faith. Out of this movement churches were established and Christianity advanced. The historic Dutch Reformed Church in the Netherlands was one of the churches. The Christian Reformed Church of the Netherlands and in the United States are both descended from the Dutch Reformed Church dated back to Reformation times. These are the roots of my faith and Christian heritage.

That influence, that message to and for the human heart and passed on to us, is the wonderful, divine blessing of redemption and forgiveness: *"Christ Jesus came into the world to save sinners."* Being one of those sinners, my goal is to let you know how this heritage has given me and generations before me assurance of forgiveness, confident hope, and principles to strive for even though we are imperfect. My prayer is that your heritage also can give you forgiveness, hope and valuable principles for your life.

Your heritage may be lost or not what you wish it to be, but God, by His grace and because of His love for you, may provide a new heritage, a new birth of freedom. Past history will not change, but you can begin a new and lasting legacy of faith for your family and generations to come, one that will prevail and not pass away.

A new birthright can supersede the old and can be gained apart from any ancestry known or unknown. You may ask, how can this be? This question was answered 2,000 years ago: *"With God all things are possible!"* As an everyday down-to-earth example, immigrants to the United States may come from a country where political freedom was curtailed and subjection to tyranny a way of life, but they gain and inherit the blessing of freedom when they settle in America and accept its customs and culture of personal liberty. So it is with spiritual heritage. When you accept a faith-filled invitation to believe, you are blessed with free salvation and participate in the heritage of Christianity.

—**Vincent G. De Young**

Introduction

A Heritage of Testing and Faith

ROOTS AND WINGS OF FAITH was partly adapted from of a section of my autobiography, IMMIGRANTS AND HAYFIELDS — *An Immigrant Family in Prospect Park (NJ),* that shares the history of the church of my youth, early years of family development, education, military service, siblings and their contributions to my life.

This work deals with the roots of my faith in the Reformation Tradition and the heritage of faith passed on by immigrant parents –"wings of faith" that had a beginning in the historical record of the Dutch Reformed Church in the Netherlands. My search for these roots has brought real meaning and understanding about my heritage and its impact on my own wings of faith. Hopefully, this story will bring redemptive blessings to the reader.

The unequal struggle by the Protestant Reformers was grounded entirely on faith in ancient Scripture because they understood that both they and the church were imperfect and needed God's Word in the search for truth. And they found truth – which gave them freedom from the oppressive powers and traditions of the established church. This declared freedom was inspired, through a spirit in their hearts, by Scripture's no-longer neglected words. Using those words, they wrote and spoke about a blessing more wonderful and greater by far than what any earthly power could grant or control - the salvation of one's soul.

Fighting the good fight and doing their work centuries ago, the Reformers deserve to be honored, named and remembered. In the attempt to do this, my focus was on John Calvin and Martin Luther. Many people today, in the whole world for that matter, are products of the Reformers' work. Beyond my own gratitude and beyond what may be comprehended, history reveals the Protestant Reformation influenced both the course of Christianity and the world for the better. Not only a part of our heritage today, it shaped the lives and values of those before us, parents, grandparents, great grandparents and past generations lost to earthly memory. My personal appreciation for what the Reformers did is expressed in and with this book.

The journey of the Reformers and the early Protestants was not easy. The recorded heritage of their sacrifice related in this book and any Christian legacy of eternal value and truth is available to all. Holy Scripture calls it new birth and a new life!

In searching for my past, a heritage was found that could not be ignored or destroyed. It was a Dutch heritage, a spiritual one filled with meaning, hard truths, surprising blessings, and eternal values. A great thing developed in my life, something that has occurred in every life – a personal heritage. It is true and has meaning and purpose. You will find part of my spiritual heritage in the this book.

The price was not cheap. As this book will show, suffering, even great suffering and agony, the lot of a Christian in this life according to Scripture, yet with the promise of eternal glory, was never absent during those years that shook the world. The simple truth of the Reformation endures: *You are saved from your sins by faith in Christ.* "The just shall live by faith!"

—Vincent G. De Young

Roots and Wings of Faith

I.
Reformation and Roots

The 500th anniversary for the Reformation was celebrated in 2017. This movement was built upon, but not limited to, Martin Luther's protest by posting ninety-five theses on the door of the Castle Church in Wittenberg Germany. At the time Luther was a little-known professor of theology whose bold and rebellious propositions were formally titled *"Disputation on the Power and Efficacy of Indulgences"* also known as 95 questions for debate.

The **Dutch Reformed Church** was created during that incredibly tumultuous period of European history known as the Protestant Reformation. In the 1500s and 1600s, numerous people, church congregations, and some countries were spurred on by ideas that broke with the established powers of the Catholic Church.

My family church, Prospect Park Christian Reformed Church, is now remembered with great appreciation and respect. It is regretful that it was not always that way in my youth and my apology is late. Little did most people know, especially young people, that the Christian Reformed Denomination with its Dutch-European roots (and other Protestant churches) had a Reformation heritage of enduring merciless and bloody persecution and distress whose great scope and duration is neither much known nor appreciated even today. It was not discussed much in church history during my attendance in Christian schools.

The Denomination had its beginnings in the early 1500's. The Protestant Reformation had two main branches - the Calvinist (also known as Reformed) branch and the Lutheran. Martin Luther, with his 95 theses, criticized the Catholic Church's sale of indulgences to enable the souls of deceased relatives to lessen or escape their time in purgatory. By implication he challenged the authority of the Church and the Pope over the Christian religion. Luther later denied there even was a purgatory.

In Europe, more than a century before, John Wycliffe in England and Jan Hus (a Czech) were early and outspoken pioneer critics of many teachings and practices of the established Church. Luther's beliefs, although much wider in scope and influence, closely resembled those of Hus. Other Protestant movements in the early 1500's also developed in Europe, sometimes independently, such as the "Anabaptists" (in their beliefs and practices they were considerably different from other Protestants and not directly related to present-day Baptists who have similar beliefs about baptism) and the followers of the Swiss reformer Ulrich Zwingli.

In the early 1500's, the Emperor of the Holy Roman Empire, that comprised much of Europe, was Charles V, who also was King of Spain as Charles I. This was the same "Emperor" before whom Luther spoke his historic refusal to recant in 1521. The Emperor, who adhered to the Catholic Church and its then beliefs and teachings, had no use for Luther or any reformer.

Most kings and queens in Europe were subject to the Emperor - so you might say Charles I (as King of Spain) was subject to himself as Charles V (Emperor)! Back then, secular rulers and authorities (kings, queens, princes, princesses, dukes, counts, etc.) were appointed or gained power, within the nobility or a "royal blood" structure in Europe, over countries and regions because of birth and ancestry, favors done or needed, power exchanges, marriages, wars, or political, religious or military intrigue. Rule over the Netherlands was granted to Spanish royalty. There was no such thing as elected or limited government then, although the Emperor himself was appointed by seven powerful and politically connected large-estate owners in Europe called "electors."

Spanish Rule. The end result of rule by Roman Catholic Spain and the Netherlands turning to Calvinism (and leaving the Catholic Church) was the incredibly harsh persecution of the Dutch population in the middle and late 1500's by their Catholic rulers.

To the dismay and extreme anger of the Spanish rulers, Protestant beliefs had developed rapidly in the Netherlands. The royal government in Spain (specifically King Charles I and later his son Philip II and those they appointed), probably fearing a loss or decrease in their power and wealth but also intending to protect Catholic dominance that served their purposes, were actually determined to exterminate the hated Calvinists from the face of the earth, but in particular from the Netherlands.

One of the duties of emperors and kings given to them when they were crowned by the Pope was to battle heresy - which they made great efforts to do – working in collaboration with Church authorities. The Reformation beliefs of the Calvinists, Lutherans and others were of course considered "heresy."

Philip II, as king of Spain, was more systematic and ruthless in his reign than his father. Just possessing a Bible was a capital offense. It is hard to believe but the Catholic Church even held that people should not have their own Bible. However, there were reasons for this – if each person could read and interpret the Bible for themselves, Church authorities believed heresies would multiply and the church would splinter into many pieces. Splintering did occur. The Church also held that translations would be erroneous and thereby cause heresies. The Reformers did not accept these reasons for banning Scripture.

II.
Calvinism and the Netherlands

Calvinism was founded on the teachings of John Calvin (1509 –1564) who was born and raised in France as a Roman Catholic. He received advanced degrees studying both law and theology. In the early 1530's, he accepted the basic principles of the Reformation movement — salvation through faith in Christ and the supreme authority of the Bible. He was influenced by earlier Reformers' teachings including Zwingli's and Luther's.

John Calvin

It was not long before Calvin became a "systematic" theologian – a leading reformer who was widely followed and admired in Northern Europe and eventually the New World. This remains true to an important extent today. To escape persecution in France, he went into exile in Switzerland where he pastored a church and did much of his extensive theological writing. In time he became the head of several churches in Geneva, Switzerland, and because of his great influence, the recognized ruler of the city itself.

Calvin and Luther were cut from the same Reformation cloth but held to important differences in some Protestant beliefs. Luther focused on faith. Calvin centered on strict Christian living along with his views on predestination. Although it follows Calvin, the Christian Reformed Church, to my knowledge, places emphasis on the Gospel, the Christian life and Christian love, also taught by Calvin. In my mind there seems to be a recognition that predestination, like God's infinite power, is beyond human understanding. It is believed because it is in Scripture, yet it is not always the center of attention. In addition to Reformed churches, many other Protestant denominations today (for example, Presbyterians and Methodists) had their beginnings in Calvinism although of course their beliefs are no longer identical to this early foundation.

This branch of the Reformation took hold early in the Netherlands. — Reformed churches based on the teachings of Calvin were organized there starting about 1540. The Dutch people, even then independent thinkers, were receptive to the principle of Scriptural authority. They enjoyed reading the newly available printed Bible for themselves. They were also attracted to the Reformers' opposition to the Catholic Church hierarchy and its corrupt practices at that time.

"Holland," "the Netherlands" and "Dutch"

"Holland" is an area that is one part of the Netherlands. Holland comprises two provinces on the

North Sea coast of the Netherlands and has the largest cities. So technically Holland and the Netherlands are not the same. However, today they are often commonly referred to by non-Dutch people as the same country. In the 1500's, "Netherlands" (literally "low countries") consisted of the present-day country plus Belgium, Luxembourg and a small part of France. It was not small back then – about the size of Illinois. The term "Dutch" (meaning "people") today refers to people living in the present Netherlands. In the 1500's, it generally referred to people in all the Low Countries. It was the Northern part of the then Netherlands (i.e. not Belgium nor Luxembourg) that became principally Calvinist (Dutch Reformed). Today of course this has changed as the nation is now mostly secular with only about 20% Protestant.

As we have seen, in the 1500's, the Netherlands was oppressively governed by the Catholic monarchy of Spain. This oppression was another reason why the Dutch were drawn to Calvinism. Why Spain ruled the Netherlands then is complicated – one could say it was basically caused or enabled by the entrenched rule of much of Europe by lines of Medieval dynastic nobility and aristocrats (mainly the Hapsburg family that started its history of royal power in the 1200's) under the overall umbrella of the "Holy Roman Empire."

For who has known the mind of the Lord?
... For of Him and through Him and
to Him are all things,
To Him be glory forever. Amen."
(Romans 11: 34, 36 NIV)

III.
Resistance and Persecution

*Submit yourselves, then, to God.
Resist the devil, and he will flee from you.*

(James 4:7 NIV)

Resistance to evil requires Divine guidance and protection. In the 1560's the Dutch began organized resistance to the extreme persecution imposed by the Spanish King and his appointees. This resistance led to the unbelievably long "Eighty Years War" (officially 1568 – 1648). The war or "Dutch Revolt" concluded, as we will see, with the independence of the northern Netherlands to which Spain finally and reluctantly relinquished its claim of dominion. It is interesting to observe that the revolt originally started simply to stop the persecution of Protestants and not to gain independence. The final result was both independence and the cessation of persecution! My father, Hendrick de Jonge, was born in the northern Netherlands in 1903, 255 years after independence.

Early in the Dutch Revolt (in the last half of the 1500's) many cities, especially in the southern and western Netherlands, had become fortresses where Calvinist rebels and citizens defended themselves against Spanish attacks.

The attacks had the following historical background. In 1555, Charles I (King of Spain and also Holy Roman Emperor) had placed the Netherlands under the rule of his son Philip II by making him King of Spain replacing his father.

Charles V, Emperor of the Holy Roman Empire
King of Spain, as Charles I

Philip's hatred of Dutch Protestants exceeded his father's - and he soon decided that all who continued to oppose Roman Catholic edicts or beliefs in the Netherlands should be put to death. He probably reasoned that if enough people were killed, the rest would save themselves by returning to the Catholic Church and loyalty to his rule. He was wrong.

In 1566, the Spanish King was provoked by marauding Calvinist mobs that invaded many Catholic churches throughout the Netherlands to smash images and icons. The people considered these to be idols - forbidden by Scripture. This "iconoclasm" may have been fueled in part by the harsh oppression of Protestants that had caused deep and bitter resentment against the Catholic Church and Spain. In any event, the Inquisition (systematic extreme torture and punishment including execution of non-Catholics and "heretics") was extended to the Netherlands with great brutality and suffering. The Inquisition was an official institution of the Church's leadership in Rome. The Spanish version was carried out by the Spanish government.

Roots and Wings of Faith

IV.

Spanish and the Inquisition

*So, whether we live or die,
we belong to the Lord.*

(Romans 14:8b NIV)

Attacks Against Protestants were serious in the Netherlands the latter part of the 1500's. The job of enforcing the policy of suppression and eradication of the Calvinist Protestants in the Netherlands was eventually given to an occupying Spanish army led by the Spanish-born Duke of Alva infamously known to history as the "Iron Duke" – what followed was the wholesale killing of thousands of men, women and children, especially in areas near the North Sea and on the Netherlands' southern border where they were vulnerable to attack.

Barbaric methods of executing Protestants (those who were caught, as many fled to Germany) were used, such as burning to death, torture, beheadings, a slashing sword, mass hangings and forced drownings under the ice. The Iron Duke committed or permitted the atrocities saying he was doing God's will.

In quelling the revolt, imposing the Inquisition, and attempting to root out the Calvinists, the Spanish army, often transported by Spanish ships and invading by sea, laid siege to rebel Dutch cities, especially those near the coast, to starve them into submission. Several cities did surrender after several months of suffering and death by starvation. But the Iron Duke violated the surrender terms that had been negotiated - and following a city's surrender he ordered or permitted the Spanish army to massacre, with ferocious, painful and bloody savagery that can hardly be described, their entire defenseless populations (those who could not escape). This was intended as a "lesson" for the rest of the country not to resist his attacks.

One of these "city victims" of the Spanish massacres (also called the "Spanish Fury") was Haarlem in the west central part of the Netherlands on the coast of the North Sea. About 2,000 Dutch people were killed there in 1573. (My mother was born in Haarlem 328 years later.) Some of the other cities where everyone was murdered after surrendering were Sutphin, Naarden, and Maastricht (about 6,000 massacred there). There were others.

Many have the idea that the Inquisition was a brief historical period in Europe where over-zealous authorities took it upon themselves to torture, in terrible ways, Protestant dissenters and other non-Catholics. According to accounts, it turns out it was much worse. The Inquisition began as a Roman Catholic institution about 1200 AD. Its purpose was to find (inquire about) and eradicate heresy or unbelief. Its method was an Inquest – the examination of suspects who were forced to go before a Church-appointed examiner or Church tribunal for their trial.

Soon after the policy was adopted, torture was approved for use during the inquest – it was used both to extract confessions (whether actually true or not) of heresy and to force witness testimony. The torture used was extreme.

If found guilty of heresy, then imprisonment, death or other severe punishment plus excommunication and confiscation of all property could be imposed on the heretic by the Inquisitors. However, Catholic Church officials arranged for infliction of the physical punishment, including the death penalty, to be handled by civic (royal) authorities. Church officials did not want blood on their hands. The death penalty was usually carried out by burning the "heretic" alive.

Inquisitors were appointed throughout Europe and sometimes sent out from Rome spreading their terror. Church authorities had extensive power in those days to impose their will.

Inquisition trials were not what we would think. An accused individual had no rights, was presumed to be guilty, and was forced by torture to confess or recant. The judges (Inquisitors) were the prosecutors – while, at the same time, they were the judges deciding guilt or innocence and also deciding the punishment to be carried out by the State. Often there was no defense counsel. Even if a lawyer was allowed and the accused was convicted, then the lawyer was also then accused of heresy – as it was a crime to both defend "heresy" and to not speak against it.

Most of the common people did not openly object to the Inquisition because, it seems, they believed as they were taught - that heresy (having beliefs not in accordance with Catholic Church official teachings, edicts, practices or traditions) should not be tolerated but rather eliminated. Tolerance seemed to be an unknown or discarded principle in those days.

If people had objections to the Inquisition, for the most part they kept silent. If they spoke up, they knew they could be victims themselves. Often, even if they kept silent, they could be accused of sympathizing with heresy for failing to report it!

During the late middle ages most people did not or could not read, or know, the Bible. It was not generally available to the common people in their language until the early 1500's. If Scripture was the final judge of heresy, they had no way of knowing what was really heresy or what was not. They, the common people, cannot be blamed for the Inquisition. Heresy as determined by Church authorities was usually considered by the people to upset the apple cart of the social, religious and power structure; that is, it interfered with life as usual, especially for those in power.

Church authorities justified the Inquisition citing Old Testament passages calling for false prophets (and also those in the towns where they lived) to be put to death. This was not a valid justification, as no Old Testament laws, events or practices overrule the New Testament's clear teachings of love and the Gospel. Old Testament history is not equivalent to God's teaching us a principle to live by in the Christian era. In any case, Protestants were not false prophets.

For the burning alive penalty, they cited a New Testament verse, John 15: 6, where Jesus stated anyone who does not remain in him is like a branch thrown into the fire and burned. But this passage in the Gospel of

John about branches being burned, in its actual words and surrounding context and in light of the rest of the New Testament, is without doubt a metaphor ("like a branch") that refers to Hell -- God's ultimate judgment of false Christians who intentionally and permanently reject Christ and the Gospel. Protestants did not reject Christ or the Gospel. The passage certainly does not in any way whatsoever say or teach that Church officials have the authority or right to direct or cause the killing or burning of any person. Someone once said, any Scripture taken out of context can be used to justify anything.

It is certainly safe to say that no amount of twisting Scripture by anyone can or should ever teach that torture and murder are Christian doctrines. In reality, it seems any "heresy," even if objectively and Biblically pure as snow, was considered a threat to those in power and treated as such in the Inquisition.

Although the Inquisition had considerable success in intimidating and suppressing dissent, so-called heretics inexorably and bravely continued to make waves over the centuries 1200 to 1600 that finally and permanently shattered Rome's iron grip on Christianity in much of Northern Europe.

The Reformation itself was the "Greatest Dissent." Martin Luther, the leading reformer, was found guilty of heresy. After he refused to recant his teachings and writings when accused while standing before the Emperor of the Holy Roman Empire in 1521, he was condemned by the Emperor as an outlaw. However, royal authorities in Germany were unable to capture him nor were they able to stop the spread of Protestant beliefs in Northern Europe.

Another example of successful dissent was, of course, the resistance of Dutch Calvinists and their final amazing success over the Spanish monarchy and its cruel brand of the Inquisition! So it is a familiar theme throughout history – the desire to be free intensifies with oppression. And liberty, especially of the holy Christian Church, cannot be stamped out from the earth!

One great historical irony is Joan of Arc. On May 31, 1431, during a period of war between France and England, she was a victim of the Inquisition - burned to death at age 19 tied hand and foot to a stake. Her crime was mainly wearing men's clothes while leading in battle and while in prison but also the "heresy" of believing God spoke to her. Her last words reportedly were "Jesus, Jesus, Jesus." The irony is that nearly five centuries later (in 1920) she was canonized as a Saint by the same Church that had caused her execution.

Note: Catholic authorities in the 1400's and the Pope himself, after protests and an appeal by Joan of Arc's family, acknowledged the error in having her executed and reversed her "guilty" verdict, 25 years after her death. It is important to point out that the Catholic authorities involved in her execution evidently were not French loyalists. Joan was.

The Inquisition was not a small thing and did not last a short time. It was practiced in one form or another for seven hundred years! It seems to have been at its worst for 450 years, from 1200 AD until the mid to late 1600's. As official policy of that Church, however, it continued into the 1900's although evidently its extreme form (torture and executions) had not been used for more than a century. It seems the last "heretic" was executed in Spain in the early 1800's. When the extremes of the Inquisition ended, Catholic authorities lost their power to dictate what others were to believe.

> It is important to emphasize that
> Roman Catholic officials today,
> as well as ordinary members of the
> Catholic Church yesterday and today,
> do not in any way share any
> responsibility or guilt for
> the past actions of the Inquisition.

Roots and Wings of Faith

V.
Dutch Victory

The Dutch City of Leiden did not surrender to a Spanish siege, even after enduring many months of anguish and starvation. Help came to this city on the North Sea coast from an unlikely source – the sea. The Dutch rebels had somehow developed a navy of sorts, more like pirates. This "navy," called Beggars of the Sea, interfered with Spanish military actions and their chain of supplies and even defeated elements of the Spanish forces on several occasions.

In 1574, the Spanish siege of Leiden was broken in what seemed a miraculous series of events. The Beggars of the Sea, following the leadership of *Prince William of Orange*, opened the dykes near Leiden and forced the besieging invaders to withdraw. The overflowing dykes, aided by the wind shifting to an Easterly direction at just the right time, had allowed supplies and assistance (for the Dutch) to be brought into Leiden. This Dutch victory sent a signal to Europe that Spanish dominance of the Netherlands was not inevitable.

The Spanish brutality imposed or allowed by their royalty continued, probably inflicting the deepest agony during three terrible days in 1576. The city of Antwerp was a great port city in Belgium, with river access to the North Sea and to world commerce. When the Spanish

Army occupied Antwerp, Belgium was then part of the Netherlands.

Perhaps angered by their low pay, or no pay, uncontrolled Spanish soldiers went on a wild killing, raping and looting rampage starting on November 4, 1576. Over three days an estimated 6,000 men, women and children, one third of the population, regardless of their faith or age were indiscriminately killed with indescribable savagery. The news of this so-called "Sack of Antwerp" sent shock waves of revulsion throughout all of Northern Europe.

Consequences came quickly for the "Sack of Antwerp" and brought final victory of the Dutch Calvinists over Spanish oppression. First, all provinces of the Netherlands immediately negotiated and signed a pact of unity in the revolt against Spanish rule and oppression. Second, England now under a Protestant, Queen Elizabeth, the First, increased its military and financial support of the Dutch. Third, Protestants in the rest of Europe now fully realized what they were up against. It seemed they became firmer in their beliefs rather than weaker, and that the Protestant cause was to endure no matter what. And Prince William of Orange became the main leader of the Dutch resistance.

Prince William of Orange, called William the Silent was born in Germany in 1533, into a family of nobility. His father was a Count. Raised a Lutheran, he became a prince as a boy on condition he receive a Roman Catholic education. As a prince, large estates were granted to him including a region in France called "Orange." Completing his education in the Netherlands, he became a Roman Catholic.

Prince William of Orange

William's leadership qualities and his nobility attracted the positive attention of both Charles I, King of Spain, and later his son Philip II who had become King in 1555. They ruled the Netherlands. William of Orange was appointed governor over several provinces in the Netherlands and was even given command of one of the King's armies.

Over time, seeing the distress and brutal continuous persecution of the Protestants, William sided with the resistance and became their leader. He did not see himself as rebelling against the King or royal authorities but as defending religious tolerance and freedom of conscience. When doing this, he initially returned to the Lutheran faith of his youth and then in 1573 joined a Reformed church in the Netherlands.

William's leadership of the Dutch resistance, however, deeply angered the Spanish King (Philip II) who saw it as treason. He targeted William for execution by anyone who could do it. A great reward was promised.

(All of William's estates and privileges as a prince were also confiscated.) After several years had passed (during this time William was the leader of the Dutch resistance), he was murdered (in 1584) by a fanatical Roman Catholic. The assassin used a pistol, a newly invented weapon, concealed in his clothing. Calvinist resistance, inspired further by the assassination of William of Orange, nevertheless continued after his death until its ultimate successful conclusion in 1648.

History now recognizes Prince William of Orange as mainly responsible for the ultimately successful uprising against Spain. Today he is celebrated as one of the heroic founders of an independent Netherlands (somewhat comparable to America's George Washington). The Dutch national anthem is about him.

In my mind, Prince William seems to be a "Moses" type, who the Lord raised up to return to the faith of his youth, going from the side of the oppressors to the side of the oppressed. Like Moses crossing the Red Sea, he eventually prevailed with the help of the "sea and the wind" to begin the rescue of the oppressed Dutch from their "bondage" to Spain. And he did not live to see their final freedom just as Moses did not live to enter the Promised Land.

Note: This William of Orange is not to be confused with another William of Orange who lived 100 years later. The later William of Orange was a prominent governmental figure in the Netherlands and also became King of England along with his English wife Mary who became Queen – the famed joint regency of "William and Mary." An American college was named in their honor.

The Dutch Revolt continued sporadically after 1576 for another 72 years (until the Peace of Westphalia)! However, during this time the worst persecutions in the Netherlands gradually subsided or were thwarted or lessened by Protestant resistance. The Dutch remained in control of most of the country and so Dutch Reformed churches continued to flourish.

After interminable years of war, in 1648 Lutherans and Calvinists were essentially made equal with Roman Catholics in their right to worship in Northern Europe. This was part of the Peace of Westphalia signed in Germany.

Dutch independence of the Northern Netherlands, which did not include Belgium and Luxembourg, was also recognized under the Peace of Westphalia. This famous Treaty, negotiated by several Northern European nations and powers, was only made possible by a long period of successful resistance by Protestants against persecution and attacks. Most of the wars against Protestants in Northern Europe thus ended in 1648!

Spain had not given up easily. In 1588, the great "invincible" Spanish Armada of 130 warships set sail to invade and conquer, for Spain, Protestant England! The intent of the King of Spain (still Philip II), with the Pope's approval and encouragement, was to restore Roman Catholic dominance in England (via Spanish control) and thereby destroy England's support of the Protestant Dutch Revolt.

Regaining domination of the Netherlands was a main objective of the Spanish planned invasion and intended conquest of England. If it had been successful, the king of Spain, Philip II, probably would have been able to resume his brutal persecution and intended extermination of Dutch Reformed Protestants.

In God's providence and within His purpose, it was not to be! The Spanish Armada was decisively defeated by the English navy (Sir Francis Drake and others) – the victory having been made possible by Drake's naval skill and an invisible hand of ocean storms and strong winds that caused the sinking of much of the Spanish fleet. Upon receiving the news of the lost sea battle, Philip II, King of Spain, reportedly exclaimed, *"I sent the Armada against men, not God's winds and waves!"* About 15,000 Spanish sailors and soldiers died in this famous battle studied by high school students - but they probably do not know that the outcome preserved the Dutch Reformed Church!

Since my ancestors were Dutch Reformed, it is quite possible my life would not exist today to share this story if the Spanish had achieved their goal! In any case, in 1588, the tide of history and God's plan had turned against Spain. Although moving slowly and haltingly, ultimate triumph decisively favored Protestant England and the Dutch Reformed Netherlands. As we have seen, independence for the Dutch was finally internationally recognized in 1648. An extremely long fight! Even before this ultimate victory, the Netherlands had begun a rapid development into a major international commercial sea power rivaling England and France!

VI
Dragonnades and Huguenots

The Peace of Westphalia in 1648 stopped the religious wars in much of Europe and the persecution of Protestants in the new "United Kingdom of the Netherlands." However, not all persecution stopped in Europe – in fact, the French government together with Catholic leaders pursued, with only a brief pause after 1648, a stern course of persecution against French Reformed Christians, often known as Huguenots.

The Huguenots were known in the 1500's and 1600's as dedicated followers of John Calvin. In those days, the late 1500's, France was marred by wars of religion due to conflicts between Catholic forces and the Protestants.

France had a long history of intermittent persecution of Huguenots starting in the early to mid-1500's. The long road of suffering by the Calvinist Christians in France did not end until 1787. Some of the methods of persecution used in France during this time seemed worse than the Spanish Inquisition if that were even possible.

The King of France, Louis the Fourteenth (XIV) - who reigned 72 years beginning in 1638 when he was five years old - was responsible for starting the new phase of French persecution of Protestants. As a child, "regents" ruled in his place. When he had matured, at age 23, he ascended the throne and took total control of France (about 1661). He was warlike, militaristic, believed in the divine right of Kings, and practiced absolute, tyrannical monarchy. Roman Catholicism was the state religion. He did not tolerate dissent of any kind and disliked Protestants (and, although he was Roman Catholic, he did not like the Pope much either). He soon determined to eliminate Protestants from France.

Louis XIV, King of France

Because the Edict of Nantes, signed in 1598 by a previous French monarch, granted a measure of tolerance to Protestants to practice their beliefs, the King's hands were tied - and he was therefore limited in what he could do to stamp out the Protestant "heretics." So, to accomplish his purpose, the King began by trying to persuade them to reconvert to Roman Catholicism. Few, if any, complied. He tried to buy their reconversions, but had no success with this effort of enticement.

Louis XIV took a major step in the early 1680's. He got the army involved and ordered French soldiers, called Dragonnades, to be stationed in Protestant homes throughout France. The Dragonnades had implicit authority to force the reconversion of the occupants. This was done by compelling people inside their homes to rejoin the Roman Catholic Church by saying "I reunite." The soldiers evidently had leeway to do what they thought necessary within the home to get this admission of reconversion. Some accounts say this included physical abuse and harassment of the families and stealing their property.

The Dragonnade "military" tactic had considerable "success" – not only in reconversions but also because many families in homes occupied by Dragonnades just abandoned their property and left France and their homes behind. Since being reconverted against their will made the process illegitimate, any reconversion was voided and they continued in their Protestant faith. Force cannot replace faith.

Then, in 1685, the frustrated French King simply abolished the existing law protecting Protestants and issued his own edict, the Edict of Fontainebleau. Thus, it became illegal to be a Protestant in France. This edict simply and immediately created a great migration of over 400,000 French Reformed Christians. They began fleeing to the Netherlands, Germany, England, and South Africa and other places throughout the Western world.

A great many of the Protestants exiting France were expert craftsmen, skilled workers, merchants and professional people that France lost to other nations. An enormous loss for France and an immeasurable gain for other countries. Some historians believe this had a permanent negative impact on France as a world power. The fleeing French Reformed Christians made a positive impact in the Netherlands and their stories of persecution apparently reinforced opposition to the Catholic Church.

My mother was a great admirer of the Huguenots. Perhaps her ancestors on her father's side living in the 1500's were French Reformed Christians.

VII.
Christians of the Desert

Some Calvinist Protestants known as "Christians of the Desert" remained in France worshipping together in secret, at night, often in open fields. Even though they worshipped in undisclosed places, their meeting places were sometimes betrayed and French authorities swooped down and arrested all present. Pastors were executed and adult men were sentenced to a lifetime of harsh slavery rowing in the "galleys" of French warships. Women were sentenced to life imprisonment, and children were taken away to be raised by Roman Catholics. This treatment and the constant persecution and cruelty nearly exceeded the vindictive brutality of the Spanish Inquisition.

By the time Protestants regained the legal right to live and worship peacefully in France in 1787, their numbers had dwindled from over a million in the mid-1500's to a few thousand. However, the Protestant faith had not died in France but in time a faithful few became firmly rooted there, mainly because of the God-given courage of "Church of the Desert" leaders. The most well-known of these Reformed leaders was Antoine Court (1696 – 1760), a shining and historic example of Christian faithfulness and fearlessness.

The persecution of French Reformed Christians reinstated by King Louis XIV was not the end of the story.

Four generations following his order in 1685, barring all Protestant beliefs in France, the whirlwind was reaped during the French Revolution (1789 –1801).

In the Revolution, the French monarchy was abolished by an angry, vengeance-seeking (against "privileged classes") hate-filled populace. In a bloody frenzy of executions committed by secularized revolutionaries, the Catholic King and Queen were, among many thousands of people, men and women, who, innocent of any crime except suspicion or rumor of not adequately supporting the Revolution, were killed by the guillotine (then thought a merciful method of killing) or butchered to pieces by street mobs after being condemned by "Revolutionary Committees." The mobs in Paris and other cities included both men and women. The leaders of the "Commune" even turned on themselves. A main leader of the Revolution, Robespierre, was himself guillotined on July 28, 1794. The extent and viciousness of the violence resulting from the French Revolution is impossible to comprehend.

Thousands of Roman Catholic clergy were murdered and thousands more sent into exile or imprisoned. The Pope himself was captured in Rome by French revolutionary military forces and locked in prison where he died. All properties of the Roman Catholic Church in France were confiscated. Roman Catholic worship and any other kind of Christian worship was prohibited by the Revolutionaries. France was essentially "de-Christianized" overnight.

In the early 1800's, after the French Revolution had spent its rage, religious freedom was again allowed. Nonetheless, France in the early 21st Century is mostly secular. Although about 50 to 60% of the approximate 65 million population identify as Catholic, a good percentage of these do not believe in God and even a larger percentage never attend church for worship. Self-identified Protestants are about 2% of the population, but a small percentage of these attend church; yet, a small minority are evangelical Christians and are active and growing. In 1985 the French government officially apologized to the descendants of the Huguenots throughout the world and acknowledged they were welcome back "home."

This long story has been told in detail about the early Reformed Christians in the Netherlands and France because it explains in part where the Christian Reformed Church and other Reformed churches originated – and why they stand for certain principles. Their origins can be traced to the Reformed churches that were forged in the fires of the "Great Persecution" 500 to 400 years ago. The roots are deep and sacred.

To this day, the Christian Reformed denomination and many other Reformed churches that have their heritage in the 1500's stand against any vestiges of the Roman Catholic Church in their doctrines, practices or physical structures. The historic impact of persecutions seemed to help create a permanent barrier. Protestant beliefs and creeds were actually reinforced in the fire and struggle of persecution, and most bridges have been burned between Protestants and the Catholic Church, at least until Christian unity is restored by God's Grace and in His time.

The New Testament records a divine purpose for persecution. In New Testament times during the First

Century, a great persecution of the first Christians broke out in Jerusalem causing them to scatter throughout the known world. Scripture clearly states that those who were scattered then "preached the word" wherever they went. The Gospel was spread far and wide. It was the same with the Reformation persecutions. They contributed to strengthening and spreading, in the following centuries, the Gospel of salvation by faith for the benefit of millions of people, even for me and my family. There also can be clearly seen a divine purpose when persecuted French Reformed Christians spread throughout the world.

According to Scripture, persecution has its own special blessings and purpose for those who suffer. Their faith will be refreshed by God, they will rejoice to share in the suffering of Christ, their afflictions will be light and momentary, their hope will not be disappointed, and they will be overcome with joy when Christ returns in glory. (1 Peter 4:12-14; Romans 5:1-5; Romans 8:38-39; and I Corinthians 4:17).

Persecution of those who believe in God also happened in the Old Testament and in other times as has been recorded for posterity. These historical events can inspire Christians with courage and encouragement to persevere. Perseverance and steadfastness were cardinal and admirable tenets of early faith-based leaders in both the Old and New Testaments.

VIII.

Scripture, Faith, Good Works

As a direct result of the Reformation and its emphasis on the supreme authority of Scripture, most Protestants have difficulty with and cannot support many Catholic doctrines; such as,

- Salvation is merited in part by good works
- Praying to Mary or any saint
- Displaying icons or images that are venerated or worshipped
- Mandatory celibacy of clergy
- The Immaculate Conception of Mary
- Calling the Pope "Holy Father" or a priest "Father"
- Belief in the Pope as the successor to the Apostle Peter
- Having priests intercede for us before God
- Purgatory and praying for the dead
- The Infallibility of official papal declarations
- Papal leadership and authority for Christians

Most Protestant churches, as a general principle, encourage a lifestyle and worship that is both compatible with Scripture and relevant to current times. Christians ought to impact culture and not the other way around (I suspect there is agreement with most Catholics on this principle). For this reason, I would submit God's Word ought to be a strong force in every Christian's life.

Concerning good works, the Catholic teaching that they in part earn salvation certainly seems logical — as it could be said this is a strong incentive for good deeds. There are several Scriptural reference that speak to the necessity of good works: *"Faith without works is dead!"* For Protestants, however, this simply means that good works will follow true faith as evidence of a changed life. The Reformation teaching is "**We are saved by faith alone.**" This faith, if it is genuine and not just a façade, is a gift of God's Grace, alive and dynamic, accompanied by and integrated with sincere repentance, confession and Baptism. It then, by God's Spirit, expresses itself in Christian love. **"By their fruits you shall know them."** Yet, is it not true we still all fall short and need continual forgiveness, encouragement, support, and renewal of our faith? And is that not a good reason to go to church?

Of course, if a person has an earnest faith in Christ (openly confesses Christ as Lord and believes in his heart Christ was raised from the dead, that is, believes the Gospel) but nonetheless also believes that good works are "necessary for salvation," there is, at least in my mind, no doubt at all he or she is still saved and is a genuine Christian. So the distance between Catholics and Protestants on this teaching may not be that great or serious.

Catholic theology on good works also has a positive impact regarding social issues with moral implications. For example, their stance on abortion is unwavering while some Protestant denominations support the right to choose abortion.

It is important to say that the emphasis on "good works," in terms of affecting human behavior, is good of course and certainly not bad – and so this emphasis on doing good should not be a cause for concern at all among Christians or anyone else. We all have a much bigger and overriding problem with people doing evil.

Concerning the belief in salvation by works, it would seem impossible to figure out how many good works are "necessary" or "sufficient" to satisfy God – and that is one reason why Protestants believe we are saved by faith alone. We do know if we have faith but we do not know about the adequacy of our works. We also believe no one can do enough works to be saved based on works - *"for all have sinned and fall short of the glory of God."* No exceptions are stated (Romans 3:23).

If we are saved by works or if faith takes a back seat to works, then extensive parts of the Bible must be thrown out and disbelieved including many passages in the Gospels of Matthew and John, the Books of Acts and Romans, the two Books of Corinthians, and the books of Ephesians, Galatians and Hebrews.

Another important point from my twin brother, Vic: Many human beings are incapable of doing any good works or it is really difficult for them – perhaps due to physical or mental illness, disability, infancy or old age, having been aborted, inherited tendencies, alcoholism, addictions and depression. Some might ask, does not this problem of incapability also apply to having faith? In true humility, it can only be said, when facing unfathomable mysteries and unanswerable questions, our only hope and sure answer and comfort is to rest on God's infinite grace, wisdom, and love in Christ. Praise His Holy Name!

Let me now close this discussion of "Scripture, Faith, Good Works." In a Bible study where every person contributed, the advantages and blessings of salvation through faith alone in Christ were listed:

1. We have no worries that we've done enough
2. It relieves stress.
3. It gives all glory to God, his grace and love.
4. It removes pride.
5. It's easy to understand and do.
6. All can be saved, that is, it's available to anyone who truly believes.
7. It forgives sins.
8. We receive the Holy Spirit.
9. It gives meaning to the Cross.
10. It removes judging by external appearances.
11. It provides equality before Christ.
12. It gives us freedom

All praise, honor and glory belong to the Lord for our salvation! Believing and confessing this, by the grace of God, through the power of the Holy Spirit, good works will then follow!

IX.

Persecution and Protestants

Before we praise Protestants too much, let me remind everyone that they were not always pillars of virtue. Both Lutherans and Calvinists, in those early days, were not models of tolerance themselves. After gaining the upper hand in Dutch provinces, Calvinists for a time did not allow Roman Catholics to practice their faith. And Dutch authorities tortured and executed, in an extremely brutal way, the man who murdered William of Orange. (According to the accounts, however, there were no systematic murders of non-Protestants in the Netherlands).

John Calvin allowed no dissent in his religious community in Geneva, Switzerland. He also was in large part responsible for the execution of at least one "heretic" by the Geneva city government. Martin Luther also condoned and encouraged a brutal governmental war against German peasants. He had accused them of misusing his doctrines to justify their violent political rebellion. Many thousands were killed in that war.

The separate sect of Anabaptists was severely and sinfully persecuted, and their devout leaders brutally killed, by both Catholics and Protestants in Northern Europe. Persecution is always a moral offense.

The scale of any persecution in those days (the 1500's and 1600's) *against* Catholics was less than the many attempts by the Church in Rome and Royal authorities to stamp out Protestants in Europe altogether. During this same time period that Dutch Reformed Christians and other Protestants in the Netherlands were being killed on a wide scale because of their beliefs, the following massacres and killings occurred in France and England:

In France, the St. Bartholomew's Day Massacre of French Reformed Christians in Paris occurred on August 24 and 25, 1572. In murderous attacks approved by the Queen Mother and the French King, about 3,000 Huguenot men, women and children were slaughtered by soldiers and mobs roaming the city. The Catholic rulers, fearful of the growing popularity and influence of the Huguenots who were seeking a share of political power, were determined to crush them. This they did.

The Louvre in Paris, on that St. Bartholomew's Day in history, was the Royal residence. Its floors and steps were covered with blood when about 30 of the King's attendants who were Protestants were slashed to death. The millions of visitors who visit the Louvre, now a great museum, probably have no suspicion of the terrible bloodshed that once happened in the halls and on steps they silently stroll gazing at art masterpieces. The bodies of many of the martyrs were thrown into the Seine and Rhone Rivers whose waters turned red with their blood.

The massacre in Paris in August 1572 triggered the almost immediate and lengthy heart-breaking murder of thousands of French Reformed Christians and their families (there is no accurate number of those who died for their faith - anywhere from 8,000 to 70,000) throughout France. This episode of severe persecution eventually slowed to a halt. After a period of about 25 years, tolerance in France was again given to Protestants in 1597 (this reprieve lasted about 80 years when severe intolerance was reinstated).

In England, in 1555, Queen "Mary Tudor" (part of the Tudor royal family and a staunch Catholic), trying in vain to reverse the tide of Protestant beliefs and to restore Catholicism to England, ordered the burning to death of Protestant leaders in England. About 300 were killed this way (though others escaped by going into exile), while many others were imprisoned or executed by beheading. This all happened during her brief five year "reign of terror." She died in 1558 after which Protestants regained control starting with the long reign of Queen Elizabeth the First, who was the half-sister of Mary Tudor.

Because of the many killings of Protestants that she ordered, history knows this Queen Mary Tudor as "Bloody Mary." While Queen of England she married, incredibly enough, Philip II, King of Spain, who we have met before. He, of course, carried out almost simultaneously, similar brute-force persecution policies in the Netherlands, including the Spanish version of the Inquisition, against Dutch Reformed Christians.

It is important to point out that England in the 1500's, during the time Protestants were in favor, had terrible episodes of persecution of Catholics – an example were the many death sentences ordered under the reign of King Henry VIII between 1530 and 1550.

It should also be strongly emphasized that great religious persecutions occurred at other times in history and not only in Europe. Of course, worst of all persecutions by far was the Nazi Holocaust, a massive and impossible-to-conceive brutal genocide committed against millions and millions of Jewish people living in Europe. Of all religious persecutions targeting Protestants since the Reformation, perhaps the worst was the Arminian Genocide in 1914 and 1915 when an estimated 1.5 million Arminian Christians (mostly Protestants) were massacred in and around Turkey and Syria.

X.
Creeds and Reformed Churches

The Reformers liked to write down their beliefs. One of their reasons was they thought that once civil and Church authorities read and understood Protestant teachings of love and peaceful obedience to civil government based on Scripture, then persecution would end. The exact opposite happened! The writings only caused more intense rage and deeper hatred. Another reason for creeds was to fill the vacuum of Bible interpretation created by the loss of Catholic authority over beliefs.

Two of the great writings that had a deep and lasting impact on the Dutch Reformed Church were the Belgic Confession and the Heidelberg Catechism (another is the "Canons of Dort"). Both were written and then adopted by Reformed churches in the 1500's, right in the middle of the worst persecutions. I listened to many sermons based on these creeds and was required to study both, especially the Heidelberg Catechism, when growing up.

The Belgic Confession

The principal author of the Belgic Confession was Guido de Pres (1522-1567). His first name is pronounced "Guydoe." He called himself "Guy." Born in Belgium (as we have seen, in the 1500's Belgium was then part of the Netherlands), he was raised a Roman Catholic by his mother. One account says she had prayed for a son who would be a great preacher. Her prayers were answered! After closely reading the Bible and the writings of Luther and Calvin, he converted to Reformation beliefs around the age of 24. Although an expert craftsman, having learned the trade of stained glass-making from his father, he followed the call to be a pastor.

Guido de Pres had the opportunity to meet John Calvin in Germany and was invited to Geneva Switzerland. He later spent two years there, one year studying directly under Calvin himself. He also learned Greek. He returned home to the Netherlands and became a pastor, preacher, and well-recognized and respected theologian. His work and activities had to be done secretly because of the ongoing persecution. He married his wife Catherine in 1559 and in the same year began work on the Belgic Confession. With the help of other Reformed church leaders and following the basic teachings of John Calvin, he completed his work in 1561. It was rapidly, that same year, accepted by all Reformed churches in the Netherlands.

The Belgic Confession, comprising 37 detailed Articles, sets forth with clear logical force the main beliefs of the Reformed faith. It states the supremacy and reliability of the Bible for revealing the Christian faith. This Confession is still, today, the principle confession of the Christian Reformed Church. It is also generally recognized as one of the great confessions of the Protestant Reformation.

Guy de Pres and Catherine had five children and seven good years together. However, he still had to work clandestinely, especially in the location where he served in Belgium. In 1567, six years after completing his work on the Belgic Confession, he was captured by the authorities and condemned to death. He was imprisoned for about eight weeks waiting execution, much of the time in a dungeon called "The Black Hole." One account says it was a sewer.

He managed to continue writing under these conditions, including a moving letter of April 12, 1567 to Catherine. The Reformed pastor and theologian, age 45, principal author of the historic Belgic Confession, was executed by hanging on May 31, 1567. Before his death sentence was carried out, he is reported to have said words to this effect: "I never dared to think that God would do me such an honor as dying for the sake of the Gospel." Nearly 378 years later, on April 9, 1945, not far from where Guido des Pres died, Lutheran pastor and theologian, Dietrich Bonhoeffer, suffered, at the hands of the Nazis, the same fate for the Gospel.

The Heidelberg Catechism

This Reformed creed was composed in Heidelberg, Germany in 1563, by a Calvinist University Professor perhaps with the help of other theologians. They were not under Spanish persecution there but of course were fully aware of the persecutions in next-door Netherlands.

A prominent Calvinist German ruler in that region was a godly man and was the human force, motivated by faith, behind this creed. His purpose was to establish comprehensive and clear answers, based on Scripture, to important questions about the Christian faith. His desire was to discern truth from error and to advance consistency and unity in teaching Biblical truths. He was especially concerned about young people knowing these truths.

As a result, the Heidelberg Catechism was written in straight-forward question and answer format, 129 to be exact. Each answer is carefully backed up with many Scriptural references. It is thorough in explaining The Apostles Creed, the Ten Commandments, and the Lord's Prayer – and their application to Christians. Martin Luther wrote a comparable catechism. Both catechisms carefully use and interpret Scripture for their principles.

The Heidelberg Catechism was quickly translated from German into Dutch. In disregard of the Spanish oppression, it was in wide use in all Dutch Reformed churches in the Netherlands by the end of 1563. It has been taken very seriously by all Reformed churches since that time – and pastors often use it as a basis for their sermons, although I cannot speak for all churches today.

Before making Profession of Faith, teenagers in Reformed Church families (both in the Netherlands and in America) for centuries, in "Catechism Class," were taught this Catechism and in many families still are. They were required to memorize many of its questions and answers. As a boy of about 14, I memorized a short form of the Catechism.

Probably the first Question and Answer in the Heidelberg Catechism is the most famous. It certainly is the most memorized.

Question: **What is your only comfort in life and death?**
Answer: **That I, with body and soul,**

both in life and death, am not my own, but belong unto my faithful Savior Jesus Christ; who with His precious blood has fully satisfied for all my sins, and delivered me from all the power of the devil; and so preserves me that without the will of the Father not a hair can fall from my head; yes, that all things must be subservient to my salvation, wherefore by His Holy Spirit He also assures me of eternal life, and makes me heartily willing and ready, henceforth, to live unto Him."

The Answer is backed up by 22 verses in the Bible! Thankfully, we did not have to memorize all of those!

It could well be the authors of the Heidelberg Catechism had the persecution, distress and death then occurring in Europe first in mind when they chose this as the first question and answer. When my sister Arlene died in 2004, Question and Answer 1 of the Heidelberg Catechism was read and was an important part of her funeral service. She of course had memorized it as a young girl.

Lutherans, Presbyterians, Methodists and many other Protestant denominations all have historical creeds and written documents of faith. All of them, along with the Reformed confessions, have their foundation strictly in Scripture and are remarkably similar, though not identical, in content and beliefs. What is more remarkable is how much they are mostly ignored today by many church pastors and members, not to mention millions and millions of non-Christians who have no knowledge or appreciation of them whatsoever. What a great revival there would be if they were once again studied, taught, preached and taken to heart. They all have great practical value for understanding and accepting both the Gospel and the incredible dimensions of the Protestant Christian faith and also for striving to live a life reflective of the Christian Faith.

XI.
Hymns and the Reformation

An important result and legacy of the Protestant Reformation was the introduction of congregational hymn singing. This heritage has been passed on through the centuries to this day, even for me. Singing hymns and sacred music has always been an important part of my life and of the churches I attended: the Christian Reformed Church, Presbyterian Church, and Lutheran Church.

In the 1500's, Congregational singing had not occurred in the Catholic church for many centuries. In Reformation times, because of the Reformers' emphasis on the importance of Scripture, most Protestant hymns were based almost literally and entirely on the Psalms. A few, however, did not strictly follow the Psalms. I have two examples – one is a Lutheran hymn and one a Reformed hymn. The Lutheran hymn is *"A Mighty Fortress is Our God."* The words of the hymn (that certainly reflect the truths in Psalm 46) and the music were both written by Martin Luther himself in the 1520's. Around the time of writing these words, Luther would probably have been burned at the stake if caught. Luther loved music. This powerful hymn of the Reformation ends with these words:

"The body they may kill, God's truth abideth still, His kingdom is forever."

The Reformed hymn is *"We Gather Together"* - originating from an unknown author in the late 1500's in the Netherlands. Also written in a time and place of great distress and trouble for Protestants, it ends with these words:

> *"Let Thy congregation escape tribulation;*
> *Thy name be ever praised!*
> *Lord make us free!"*

This hymn is now frequently sung by many Protestant denominations at the time of Thanksgiving.

Both of my parents sang in the church choir until they were not physically able to participate in a choir. He a strong tenor, she a talented alto. But even in their 80's they continued to join in singing hymns in church with great enthusiasm. I also have had the privilege of participating, as a tenor, in church choirs since my early 30's.

Congregational hymn singing in the Christian Reformed denomination is special and can even be overwhelming. The power, force and sheer thunderous volume of everyone's enthusiastic participation has to be experienced to be believed and appreciated.

It is hard to understand why any Christian would not want to join in with all their heart and soul when hymns are sung in church (I am referring to " sing - able" hymns of course – some hymns are difficult or even impossible to sing, at least the first few times). Before writing this book, I had written a devotional that shows what I believe about singing hymns. Here is that devotional (never seen before or published).

Sing to the Lord

From the first days of Christianity and even well before that, more than 3,500 years ago in the Old Testament (Exodus 15:1), singing has been a vital part of a God-fearing life and worship. In the record of the night Jesus was betrayed, we are told that just before He and his disciples left the upper room, they sang a hymn (maybe one of the Psalms set to music). See Mark 14:26, Matthew 26:30. This included our Lord himself participating in singing a hymn! On the night of His betrayal no less!

And while other prisoners listened, the Apostle Paul and his missionary companion Silas, after being whipped, prayed and sang hymns at midnight, while in prison and with their feet in stocks, in the city of Philippi during the first century A.D. (Acts 16: 25). Stocks are extremely uncomfortable to say the least, even continuously very painful (especially after being flogged!) - so that not singing in church because it is "uncomfortable" or "not for me" or "I don't feel like it" is hardly supported by the Bible!

The Bible has many other references to singing, especially the Psalms which were written 3,000 years ago, about 1000 BC. Many Psalms were specifically written by David and others in order to be sung. David, a musician, was known as the "Singer of Israel." With this history, it's no wonder that most churches make congregational singing and choirs of all kinds an important and even essential part of worship services.

When singing is mentioned in Scripture, it is frequently in the imperative sense. The Bible not only encourages but commands us to sing! One example is Psalm 30:4 that reads" Sing to the Lord you saints of his; praise his holy name." A New Testament passage, Ephesians 5:19-20 is clear about it: "Speak to one another with psalms, hymns and spiritual songs. Sing and make music in your heart to the Lord, always giving thanks to God the Father for everything, in the name of our Lord Jesus Christ." Like branches are one part of a tree, singing hymns is one part of the Christian life.

Some have the idea that if they feel they can't (or don't wish to) carry a tune, it's ok to attend church but not participate at all in any hymn. This seems a bad use of the word "can't." And it would seem to set a visible "not a good idea" example for the young and also for members and guests in church.

Think about it. Many hymns are really moving and wonderful prayers and others are magnificent, inspiring songs of praise to the Lord. Christian hymnbooks in reality are a precious collection of pearls of great price -- the result of Scripture-based, mountainous, and Spirit-inspired effort by composers, authors, editors and publishers. Have they wasted all of that as far as you are concerned?

Singing hymns and spiritual songs is also a strong witness for Christ. You are expressing your faith for all to hear! If you can hum even the simplest tune or sing "Happy Birthday," then surely you can join in singing a hymn to the Lord. Anyone who has a voice can sing! Even the smallest child can do it - and is eager to do it!

Sing to the Lord!
Sing to the Lord a new song;
Sing to the Lord, all the earth.
Sing to the Lord, praise his name;
Proclaim his salvation day after day.

(Psalm 96:1-2 NIV)

Roots and Wings of Faith

XII.
Persecutions and Meaning

Persecution is a serious wrong and it always has been regardless of who was being persecuted and who was doing the persecuting.

Much of the world uses torture in persecution, causing great pain, suffering and anguish. In today's world it includes harassment, intimidation, bullying, discrimination and ridicule. Victims are those who simply are different or weaker than the perpetrator.

Christians are now persecuted by some governmental authorities in the name of law and order. These authorities seem to be following an agenda of suppressing the practice or teaching of peaceful religious beliefs that harm, intimidate or harass no one. For example, a perfectly commendable statute prohibiting sex discrimination might conceivably be applied to a Christian school that has separate bathroom facilities for the sexes, thereby compelling the school to have unisex bathrooms.

Christians, of course, agree that all persecution is wrong, but they also have the perspective of being persecuted themselves. Let me then express some thoughts about the meaning and impact of the events described in this book and what has been learned from my heritage.

- Each person has to come to grips with their own feelings and reaction when realizing the suffering and agony that actually happened in the Great Persecution of Protestants. For me, my first emotions when reading the historical accounts were shock with deep sadness. These people after all were brothers and sisters in Christ – who believed then almost exactly as I do now.

- My next feeling was overwhelming gratitude and respect for their paving the way so that today no single authority can dominate or stop peaceful religious belief and peaceful religious practice in America! This freedom of religion and worship now enjoyed, that came with a costly historical price, is fragile and may not be permanent. It calls for vigilance and prayer.

- It is also true that we are no better or more deserving than those who were persecuted in the past. It could happen again and is presently happening with Christians in the Middle East and many other places. In this world, suffering and experiencing persecution, even death, because of faith in Christ is not outside the will of God. Jesus Himself told us this truth. And every freedom we have now could suddenly be taken away. As we have seen, God also has His own divine purposes for the suffering of Christians that may not be discernible to us.

- A Christian's life on earth is a pilgrimage, whether short or long. We become so concerned with our lives, our health, our well-being, living longer, our education, our status, our physical security, all our worries and problems – so much so that we forget our true home (and those of our household) is with the Lord. One of my aunts who suffered here on earth has this inscription on her tombstone: *"With Christ."*

- Our life is eternal – for Christians it does not stop with death. Jesus told us this. He also told us not to be afraid and to not fear those who can kill the body but not the soul; that God loves his own and holds them in His Hand. We need so much to hold firmly and convincingly to this truth as did faithful Christians before us.

- Because we were born prone to sin, all of us are readily capable of doing really bad things. We know in our hearts this is true. For this reason, we are not worthy of judging those who committed the acts of the Great Persecution. That is for God alone. We also know that even people who know the Bible and identify as being "Christian" can fall into, or lapse into total blind apathy concerning, great sins of bitter and uncontrolled hatred, murder, and shocking atrocities. Millions of German Protestants (not all by any means) willingly and even with enthusiasm followed Hitler down a path of great and dark evil. Considering the incredible fiery destruction of Germany in 1945, he led them into the halls of hell on earth.

- As mentioned before, present-day Catholics are not at fault in any way for the Great Persecution – just as present-day Germans are not at fault for the evil and immense crimes of the Nazis. The Bible is not ambiguous about this: *"The son will not share the guilt of the father..."* (Ezekiel 18:20). In the year 2000, Pope John Paul II, on behalf of the Roman Catholic Church, essentially apologized for the Inquisition and its cruelties over many centuries. He previously had acknowledged the wrong of the St. Bartholomew's Day massacre of French protestants in Paris that occurred in 1572.

- Forgiveness, just as love, is an important and necessary Christian virtue – and must be applied and always practiced as the Lord taught us and set the example for us, even on the Cross. *"Father forgive them, for they know not what they do."* Vengeance and hatred have no setting at the Christian's table.

- It is for us of course, as the successors to those who suffered and died for the Gospel, to live up to the principles of the Protestant faith – always trusting in the Bible, as God's Word, following the great creeds and confessions, and never forgetting to stand for freedom, peaceful beliefs, worship and forgiveness.

- And we know, based on history, that a point can be reached when firm resistance, relying on God, is necessary. This resistance is necessary against those who hate freedom and violently attack us, our families and friends. This justifiable defense, as we have seen, happened with the Dutch revolt and with the defeat of the Spanish Armada. It also was plain to see in World War II and in many other times in history.

- Anyone can believe what they want to and any religion can have any belief. Yet should we not in our own land take a stand, as did our forefathers, against any religion, sect or philosophy whose main intent and purpose includes wanton violence against others, whose practices definitely inflict physical harm or abuse, or who exert control or destroy freedom by using violence and force?

Let me now conclude this work with the following passages of Holy Scripture, words that will never pass away. May these be stored in your heart on that day, the day meant for you and for each one of us, when the Lord calls us to our eternal home.

> *To you, O Lord, I lift up my soul;*
> *In you I trust, O my God.*

(Psalm 25:1-2 NIV)

> *Believe in the Lord Jesus and you will be saved –*
> *you and your household.*

(Acts 16:31 NIV)

> *I wait for the Lord, my soul waits,*
> *and in His word I put my hope.*

(Psalm 130:5 NIV)

Roots and Wings of Faith

About the Author

Vince G. De Young, MBA, JD, is a retired attorney now living in Kentucky. He and his twin brother, Victor, were born in Paterson, New Jersey, and raised in nearby Prospect Park. Their parents, Henry De Jonge and Jemima De Jonge (nee De Waal Malefyt), were both

immigrants from the Netherlands, Jemima coming as an infant in 1902 and Henry as a 19-year old twenty years later.

Along with their two brothers and three sisters, Vince and Vic were brought up in the Christian Reformed Church, graduating from a high school in New Jersey affiliated with that church. They went on to attend Calvin College in Grand Rapids, Michigan. After two years Vic stayed at Calvin College, but Vince returned to New Jersey and graduated from Fairleigh Dickinson University with a B.S. Degree. Following graduation, he entered the U.S. Air Force and served as a Navigator four and half years. He met and married his wife, Carol, while in the Air Force.

After military service, Vince received his law degree from the University of Texas. His legal career was mostly in business law, first as an Associate for Simpson Thacher and Bartlett in New York City; then a Senior Attorney for KFC Corporation in Louisville, Kentucky; and then as Associate General Counsel for Holiday Inns, Inc., and Harrah's Entertainment, Inc. in Memphis, Tennessee.

During his career, he also had a private law practice for five years. While in Louisville, he served as an Adjunct Professor of Law for the University of Louisville. While working in Memphis, he received his MBA. In later years Vince and Carol moved to Michigan where he had his own law practice and taught Business Law.

Vince and Carol have been members of the Lutheran Church (Missouri Synod) for 24 years. Previously, they were Presbyterians. Married 56 years, they have been blessed with raising six children, Donna, Cindy, Mary, John, Rebecca and Shannon, and further blessed with nine grand-children. Carol, a nurse by profession, stays busy with mission trips and mission work, grandchildren, and church activities. Vince participates in the church choir, leads a Bible Study and helps out with the church's preschool. He also assists Carol with the grandchildren and plays golf with his brother Vic who usually beats him.

Vince is the author of, "No Brighter Dawn" (2012) about Paul Revere and the Battle of Lexington. This work, Roots and Wings of Faith, is his second book and in the works is IMMIGRANTS AND HAYFIELDS, an autobiography story of his immigrant family in Prospect Park (NJ). His twin, Vic, is author of "These are a Few of my Favorite Memories" (2001) about their youth in Prospect Park.

Afterword

In 1934, a 35-year-old American Baptist Minister, boarded a ship bound for Europe. His journey took him to several countries until he reached his destination in Berlin, a conference of Baptist ministers. The curtain of Nazi evil had not yet fully descended on Germany. While there, he learned more about the Protestant Reformation and the protest of Martin Luther 417 years earlier that had changed the world. It made a difference to Michael King. So much of a difference that when he returned to America, he changed his first name and the name of his son, Michael, Jr., to Martin Luther. The rest of the powerful and nation-changing story of Dr. Martin Luther King, Jr. is now recorded in history

In many different ways the Reformation has power, power for good. As realized by the senior Martin Luther King and his son Martin Jr., it certainly stands for freedom and the right to protest, using nonviolence, against discriminatory restrictions on freedom and against the suppression of equal rights under law.

In our day and time, the Reformation also stands for holding fast to the Scriptural truths Christians believe despite the attacks on Christianity and its peaceful practice. These attacks in America often take the form of lawsuits and media ridicule, (and could be worse) but that should not be surprising – because persecution of Christians is forewarned in Scripture. The Protestant heritage, then, has meaning for this environment today – telling us not to be Christians only in secret. After all, we are children of the Reformation and the persecutions that were suffered then. We know what they went through, that it can be tough to be a Christian.

The Reformation provided many legacies that are meaningful and lasting blessings. The most important one, handed down to and through Protestant denominations, is that salvation cannot be purchased. It is by faith in Christ that individuals are saved from sin. This faith, which is free and gives us forgiveness and freedom, is not just knowledge or belief that Jesus lived; it is a certain and sure conviction that He died and rose again, for you and anyone who would truly believe. In my life, forgiveness has included a harsh yet wonderful earthly reality. When trapped, like the Prodigal Son, in the consequences of mistakes and foolishness, unwanted painful events lifted me up –and by God's grace alone restored my senses. All thanks be to God! The third verse of this old Irish hymn by H. W. Baker (1821-1877) says it well:

> *"Perverse and foolish, oft I strayed,*
> *Yet in love He sought me.*
> *And on His shoulder gently laid, And*
> *home, rejoicing, brought me!"*

For those churches and members who may have strayed from the foundation of salvation by faith, it would be important, I respectfully submit, to return to it. For the Reformation and its persecutions showed that the Christian hope is directed toward forgiveness and the gift of eternal life through faith.

The Reformation, it is important to add, did not teach that faith is an easy way out. Freedom given by faith is not freedom to sin but freedom from sin - freedom from both its guilt and its power to control and condemn. Sincere faith motivates and turns life in the opposite direction of sin. And Scripture, by its authority, instructs us what is sin and what is not. This is what the Reformers taught.

A second Reformation legacy is the supreme religious authority of Scripture over traditions, opinions of people, and decisions of organizations. The Gospel given to us is simple, even a small child understands "Jesus loves me." Yet, Scripture is long, not just a pamphlet or slogans. Many passages are not self-explanatory in their meaning. They must be explained. The Reformers gave guidance on this – that a verse or passage must be interpreted, with the aid of God's Spirit, in light of its surrounding text, its original language, and in light of other teachings in both Testaments, knowing that the New Testament prevails over the Old. Scripture verses are not to be taken out of their context nor should their meaning be misused by human intellect.

Believers are not Lone Rangers in Bible interpretation. The Protestant Creeds, another legacy of the Reformation and a great blessing, already explain and bind together much of Scripture, its message of salvation, and the Christian life. Most questions have already been answered. For example, there is no need to debate the divinity of Christ, whether Christians can go directly to God in prayer, whether there is judgment after death, whether people are sinful and need forgiveness, whether as individual Christians we should be kind and forgiving, or whether Christ is coming again.

It is true the Creeds of Protestant churches differ in interpretation of some principles, but these differences relate primarily to points of non-salvation beliefs. As an example, faith in Christ is essential for salvation, but believing in a particular method of church practice is not. Consequently, it is respectfully suggested that Protestant Creeds, born in persecution, should not be ignored but rather renewed, preached and followed.

A last Reformation legacy to mention, important to me, is Singing! The thousands of hymns written after the Reformation are treasures for the centuries. Hopefully all Christians would take advantage of the blessings of hymns that have been freely given to us at great cost to faithful writers and composers.

For my life and family, the search for heritage revealed many blessings. The guidance of parents began the stream. Then there were struggles, mistakes and hard times that, by God's grace, turned into underserved blessings. Starting from earliest youth, the churches attended, without me fully realizing it, offered great blessings of the Reformation: Faith that gives assurance of forgiveness and eternal life; Scripture and Creeds that, with the wisdom and help of faithful pastors, guide our lives; and hymns that calm our fears and comfort our souls. May this also be true for you! You may ask, where is love in all this. God's love is the source of faith and overcomes all things. We love because He first loved us.

—**Vincent G. De Young**

Publisher's Appendix:
Bible Translations And Differences

The Bible of the Reformation

One of the most historically significant translations of the Bible into the English language was the **Geneva Bible**, preceding the King James Bible by 51 years. It became known as the **Bible of the Reformation** and the one used by the early colonists fleeing oppression from Europe. Printing of the Geneva Bible stopped in 1644 due to exclusive rights given to the Royal Printers for the King James Bible. Most American Protestants embrace the KJB without knowing that ninety (90) percent of the 1611 text is the same as the Geneva Bible. The ten percent difference is the problem.

Scripture Means Exactly and Only

Holy Scripture means exactly and only what the first people who heard it understood it to mean. The pristine believers read a circulated portion of sacred writings once to a gathered group who understood the meaning of each word. They understood because it was in their language and culture. Then that portion was exchanged with another group. Remember, this was before the printing press and all writing was done by quill on parchment. Paul sent with his letter to the Colossians these directions:

And when this letter is read among you, send it to be read also in the assembly of the Laodiceans; and that you likewise read the letter from Laodicea. (Colossians 4:16 EDNT)

Translation Problems

The basic problem with a translation occurs when one translates from a language and culture into another language and/or culture. Academia is clear: when one translates from a language and culture to another, the meaning (understanding) changes. The primary difference in the Bibles used by Roman Catholics and Protestants is the root language used and the cultural environment both when originally written and again when translated. The Hebrew and Aramaic parts of the Bible were translated as the Latin Vulgate, while the *Koine* Greek and some Aramaic was translated into English. Catholic scholars used the common Latin to translate into English, while the English academics used *Koine* Greek to arrive at an English version of sacred Scripture. A foundational problem was the original language of scripture was structured to reach the common people who understood the meaning of each word.

Paul and Luke each wrote one-fourth of the New Testament and they were the two best educated men in the pristine church. So, education or academics is not the problem. The difficulty is the change in language and culture. These two men were chosen of God to reach the Gentile world, because they knew both the languages of the day and were exposed to the various cultures of the time.

In an effort to widen the scope of circulation of Sacred Writings, translations were made into classical or academic languages. Historically, both common Latin and common Greek were translated into academic English for the educated class. This is where the problem started. Men unable to control their bias began to interpret scripture with the intent to influence doctrine rather than a basic relationship with God and man.

Academia was influenced by sectarian perspectives and began to develop language to either protect the stated church or influence a particular class of people. It was a road filled with good intentions, but failed to consider the purpose of scripture: to speak to the common folk. When this failed, undereducated men began to take it upon themselves to explain and interpret the intent of scripture without adequate language training or clear cultural understanding of the context of words.

Language and Cultural Differences

This partially explains the language difference; however, the culture and traditional difference in the finished product depended on the bias of the translator. A basic rule of data, as accepted in academia, is *"All data contains error."* Why is this true? Because it is handled by human beings who are imperfect and have difficulty controlling their bias.

Early English Translator Problems

The first hand-written English language Bible was translated in the 1380's by John Wycliffe, an Oxford professor, scholar, and theologian. He was well-known throughout Europe for his opposition to Catholic teaching.

Wycliffe translated out of the Latin Vulgate, which was the only source text available to him. The stated Church was so infuriated by the English translation, that 44 years after Wycliffe's death, the Pope ordered his bones dug-up, crushed, and scattered in the river! It then became common practice to execute translators of the Bible.

About 150 years later, Pope Clement VII in anger excommunicated Henry VIII in 1533. The next year the Act of Submission of the Clergy removed the right of all appeals to Rome, effectively ending the Pope's influence in England. The first Act of Supremacy confirmed Henry by statute as the Supreme Head of the Church of England (1536). Only three years later Henry VIII authorized the Great Bible (1539) for circulation.

The Christian Old Testament overlaps with the Biblical Hebrew, Aramaic and the Greek Septuagint. The Hebrew Bible is known in Judaism as the Tanakh. The New Testament, a collection of inspired writings by early Christians, mostly Jewish disciples of Jesus, except Gentile Luke, were written in first-century *Koine* Greek during the great missional expansion of early Christianity.

The King James Bible (1611) was based on six previous English translations, but there were seven. The Douay-Rheims translated by Catholic scholars from the Latin Vulgate and sanctioned by the Roman Catholic Church (1582) was the seventh. The existing and available English translations in 1611 were:

1. **Tyndale's Bible** (1526) by William Tyndale, the first English translation directly from Hebrew and Greek texts. Tyndale was arrested in 1535 and executed in 1536.

2. **Coverdale's Bible** (1535) compiled by Myles Coverdale who published the first complete Bible in English, he was also involved in the Great Bible of 1539. He died in 1569.

3. **Matthew's Bible** (1537) published by John Rogers under the pseudonym "Thomas Matthew," it combined the New Testament of William Tyndale, and as much of the Old Testament as he had been able to translate before being captured and put to death.

4. **Great Bible** (1539) was the first authorized edition of the Bible in English, since the Tyndale Bible was incomplete. Myles Coverdale translated the remaining books of the Old Testament for publication. Henry VIII overthrew papal authority and authorized the Great Bible.

5. **Geneva Bible** (1560) known as the **Bible of the Reformation** was translated by a colony of Protestant scholars in exile from England. They worked under the direction of Miles Coverdale and John Knox and were influenced by John Calvin. The New Testament completed in 1557; the Old Testament in 1560.

6. **Bishop's Bible** (1568). Archbishop of Bishop of Canterbury, Matthew Parker, led a committee of Bishops in the translation. Their initials appear at the end of their separate work.

7. **Douay-Rheims Bible** (1582) was translated from the Latin Vulgate by Oxford Catholic scholars working in exile overseas, while back in England reformers were trying to overthrow the foundations of the Catholic church. Their work was published New Testament (1582) and Old Testament (1560) by Catholic colleges in Rheims and Douay, hence the name Douay-Rheims.

Nearly four centuries later in the 1940's another Oxford Catholic scholar, Mgr. Ronald Knox, Theologian and former Anglican Priest (1912-1917) who converted to Catholicism during World War I, translated an authorized Catholic version from the Latin Vulgate at a different time in world history – the closing years of World War II. His work was published in 1945.

The similarities and differences further explain the translation difficulties. It appears in both cases the translators were University of Oxford trained Catholic scholars. The Douay-Rheims group were products of centuries of Catholic tradition. On the other hand, Mgr. Ronald Knox, was a convert to Catholicism. However, the Church of England had strong Catholic associations which remained in place and influenced both dogma and order. In the present United Kingdom, many English Catholics presently use the King James Version of the Bible, rather than the authorized version: Douay-Rheims.

(8) **King James Bible** (1611) This would make the King James Version, the eighth (8th) in this line of early English translations of the Bible. When Queen Elizabeth I died in 1603, a draft act was in Parliament for a new version of the Bible: "An act for the reducing of diversities

of bibles now extant in the English tongue to one settled vulgar [common] translated from the original." King James in 1640 decreed that no Bible could be printed in English in the British Empire except the KJB, which in reality was also a Catholic Bible published to compete with the Latin text and the English Douay-Rheims Bible.

Any difficulties found in the Authorized (1611) King James Bible (KJB) were not the fault of classical scholarship, but the restrictive and nonacademic instructions given the translators by Royalty and the many provisions for individuals to change their work. Indeed the KJB was a Church of England document limited by the culture and nature of the English language. Most are not aware of the many changes made to the 1611 text; mainly between 1613 and 1904. These changes in the KJB are why it is now called King James Version (KJV).

The original changes were to correct typographical errors, add notes, and omit the Apocrypha between the Testaments, but there has always been scholarly opposition in the process. This produced more translations and more versions. Few realize that the Church of England now recommends six (6) versions in addition to the 1611 text.

Words in 1611 did not mean the same as a Modern English language reader understands today. The KJB was produced in Early Modern English or better known as Elizabethan or Shakespearean English. The language was still in transition until about 1650. For example, when Queen Elizabeth I died in 1603, a draft act was in Parliament for a new version of the Bible: "a new translation in the English to one settled vulgar translation." Note the word "vulgar" at the time of the KJB meant "common or popular" but has a different connotation in the vernacular of today. Who would purchase a "vulgar" edition of the Holy Bible today?

In recent decades many translators have produced multiple versions of the Bible. Each used slightly different academic and theological (sectarian) perspectives. This ranges from a word-for-word literal translation, to a formal language equivalent, a mixture of formal and functional equivalent and a meaning based functional equivalent approach. My own approach in a 42-year effort to produce a candid rendering of the Greek New Testament in common English was to use an original intent-meaning and modified functional based language equivalent process to produce The EVERGREEN Devotional New Testament (EDNT). It is published and distributed by 30,000 distributors in 100 countries.

— **Hollis L. Green, ThD, PhD, DLitt**

_____

Secure a copy www.gea-books.com/bookstore *or the Expresso Book Machine© or anywhere good books are sold.*

Suggested Reading And References Bibliography

Bainton, Roland. *Here I Stand*

Brecht, Martin. *Martin Luther* (3 vols)

Camereon, Euan. *The European Reformation*

Colish, Marcia. *Medieval Foundations of the Western Intellectual Tradition, 400-1400*

Durant, Will. *The Reformation* (1957) Simon and Schuster, New York.

Euan Cameron, *The European Reformation --The Sixteenth Century*

Gäbler, Urich. *Huldrych Zwingli: His Life and Work*

Ganoczy, Alexandre. *The Young Calvin*

Gonzalez, Justo L. (2010).*The Story of Christianity, Volume II: The Reformation to the Present Day,* Harper Collins

Hall David W. and. Lillback, Peter A .*A Theological Guide to Calvin's Institutes*

Kolb , Robert and, Charles P. *The Genius of Luther's Theology*

Kolb, Robert. *Martin Luther: Confessor of the Faith*

Lindbeerg, Carter. *The European Reformations*

Lindberg, Carter. *The Reformation Theologians*

Locher, W. *Zwingli's Thought: New Perspectives*

Lohse, Bernhard/*The Theology of Martin Luther*

MacCullloch, Diamaid. *The Reformation —A History*

Marius, Richard. *Martin Luther*

Martin Luther, edited by John Dillenberger

Martin Luther's Basic Theological Writings, edited by Timothy Lull

Marty, Martin. *Martin Luther: A Life*

McKim, Donald. *The Cambridge Companion to Martin Luther*

Metaxas, Eric. *Martin Luther: The Man Who Rediscovered God and Changed the World*

Oberman, Heiko. *The Harvest of Medieval Theology*

Parker, H.L. *John Calvin —- Calvin's Preaching*

Selderhuis, Herman. *John Calvin: A Pilgrim Life*

Shelley, Bruce, *Church History in Plain Language*

Steinmetz, David C. *Luther in Context*

Stephens, P. *The Theology of Huldrych Zwingli*

Wendel, Francois. *Calvin: Origins and Development of His Religious Thought*

A Word of Blessing

"And the God of all grace,
who called you to His eternal glory in Christ,
after you have suffered a little while,
will Himself restore you and make you
strong, firm and steadfast.

To Him be the power
for ever and ever.

Amen!"

I Peter 5:10 -11 NIV

www.ingramcontent.com/pod-product-compliance
Lightning Source LLC
Chambersburg PA
CBHW030003050426
42451CB00006B/100